Modern Family Trivia

Quotes, Facts, Q&A about The Sitcom
Modern Family

10 Quotes About Relationships
1. The Hero In My Family Is My Family, Because Of Who We Are Together.

When Manny had to write an assignment about who the hero in his family was, he was at a crossroads. Sure, it was incredibly entertaining to watch him cross people off the list as he witnessed some of their pettiness and more juvenile side. But the best quote came at the very end of the episode.

Manny realized that even though they were all completely different, at the end of the day, as a unit, they were powerful. They were strong. And they were all heroes because no matter what, at the end of the day, they're always there to be heroes for each other.

2. Family Is Family. Whether It's The One You Start Out With, The One You End Up With, Or The Family You Gain Along The Way.

One of the best things about Modern Family is the way it depicts, well, a family. Behind this quote from Gloria there is a beautiful sentiment that we should all get behind. Because while many people are lucky to be born into a family that they love, others are not so blessed.

But the good thing is, family is not just about blood. Family is about love, and you get to choose who you want to be your family. Gloria, Manny, Cam, Phil, and Lily, all came into the Pritchett's lives later on. And now, look at them - they are one crazy bunch, as Jay would say, but a wonderful, loving one.

3. The Ones Who Will Love Us Without Judging? Who Forgive Our Faults And Celebrate Our Imperfections?

The entire quote by Gloria goes like this: "It's scary to let people see the real you, even when these people are your own family. But aren't they the ones we should be least worried about? The ones who will love us without judging, who forgive our faults and celebrate our imperfections, maybe even encourage us to let our true selves shine through".

And what a lovely sentiment it is. Because at the end of the day, those who love you, love you for who you are. You don't have to be afraid of not being perfect, because that's not what they want you to be. They just want you to be you - and they'll be there to make sure you are your true self.

4. It's Gonna Be Tough To Say Goodbye… It Always Is. Nobody Loves Change. But Part Of Life Is Learning To Let Things Go.

Saying goodbye is an inevitable part of life. Whether it is saying farewell to a good friend that is moving away or a child that is off to begin a new chapter of their lives, learning how to let go is a necessary part of our existence.

And Phil knows that, just like he knows that it's okay. Because a little way down the road, you'll see them again. Or if it's a permanent goodbye, they will always have a place in your heart.

5. Sometimes Things Work Out Just The Way You Want. Sometimes They Don't. But You Have To Hang In There Because 90% Of Being A Dad Is Just Showing Up.

What makes a good parent? That is a question everyone who's ever had children asks themselves over and over again. There is no rulebook for this - that would simply be too easy.

Jay seems to have it somehow figured out. At the end of the day, even if there's a situation you don't know how to deal with, what matters is that you show up and be there for your kids.

6. You See, The Dreamers Need The Realists To Keep Them From Soaring Too Close To The Sun. And The Realists, Well, Without The Dreamers, They Might Never Get Off The Ground.

The notion that opposites attract has neves made more sense than when Cam said this and left us thinking. Yes, in many ways, some of us are dreamers and some of us are realists.

They key in a good, loving relationship is learning how to use each others' strengths to propel the other one forward in life, even if you don't agree in some aspects.

7. Making A Child Is The Easy Part. The Hard Part Is Everything That Comes After.

The idea of having children can be quite terrifying, even if you're a stage in your life where everything seems to be steady - finances, emotions, and support systems.

But it's still scary. Because it's a little piece of you that will be running around the world for the rest of your life. But it's a small price to pay for the joy you'll feel.

8. We're From Different Worlds, Yet We Somehow Fit Together. Love Is What Binds Us Through Fair And Stormy Weather.

Much like one of the first quotes we went through, this one shares the same beautiful sentiment about family, and how the family that you end up with can be the family you choose.

It doesn't matter where each of you comes from or if you don't share the same DNA. Because what defines family is simply love

9. We Do Strange Things For The People We Love. There May Be Bumps Along The Way, But We Never Stop Wanting The Best For Them. That's What Makes It Such A Tough Job, But The Best Job In The World.

Claire gave us this quote when she let Phil win a race after he had a bad day. And while she is not promoting dishonesty, she's making light of something very true - that we do really weird things for those we love.

Sometimes, it's not easy. Pride has to be set aside, egos get wounded...but it's all part of the job description for one of the best jobs in the world.

10. Those Fears You Never Get Past. So Sometimes All You Have To Do Is Take A Deep Breath, Hold Them Close, And Hope For The Best.

This was Phil reflecting about fears, and how you do get over them. But the only fears you never get over are those pertaining to your children and the outside world, a world you very often can't protect them from.

This is something every parent has to accept at some point - that your kids are yours, but not really. They'll be hurt and you won't be able to stop it from happening. But just like Jay said, you have to keep showing up. Be there for your children, and hope for the best.

10 Things about Modern Family

1. Luke Dunphy is a genius

On the show, Luke isn't the brightest bulb but in real life, actor Nolan Gould is a genius. The actor revealed on the Ellen DeGeneres Show that he is a Mensa member and has an IQ of 150.

2. Julie Bowen was pregnant with twins in the pilot

When the pilot episode was being shot, Julie Bowen was pregnant with twins. She was right for the part and the makers went ahead with her though they had to strategically place objects in front of her so her belly could be hidden on the show.

3. Joey could have been Phil?

Matt LeBlanc aka Joey from Friends was in line to do Phil Dunphy's part which eventually landed in the lap of Ty Burrell. The makers considered Craig T Nelson for Jay Pritchett's part, but Ed O'Neill bagged the role.

4. Fizbo isn't a Modern Family character

Cameron's clown character Fizbo made an appearance in the early seasons of the show and was a part of the storyline throughout. But as revealed by actor Eric Stonestreet, Fizbo wasn't created by Modern Family writers. On the Today show, Eric revealed that Fizbo was the name given to his clown character by his father when he was just 9 years old. His grandmother made the costumes and Fizbo often performed at kid's birthday parties.

5. Modern Family cast is quite like a real family

top 10 modern family episodes Modern Family cast members were nominated in the supporting categories throughout the run.

During the early seasons of the show, the cast made a pact that they will submit themselves for supporting parts in award shows as the show is an ensemble and does not have any lead actors.

6. Mitch and Jesse have something in common

On Oprah's Next Chapter, Jesse Tyler Ferguson revealed that he had to come out thrice to his own father. The writers of the show borrowed this tidbit from his life and modeled Mitchell's character on it. On the show, we are told that Mitch had to come out to Jay multiple times.

7. Ariel Winter's familial issues

Ariel Winter was legally emancipated from her mother when she was 17. The actor spoke about this on The Ellen DeGeneres Show and revealed that she was under her sister's guardianship for a while but was fully independent before she turned 18. Allegedly, Ariel's mother had spoken ill of her on numerous occasions and also caused some problems on the Modern Family set.

8. First primetime gay-kiss

In 2010, a Facebook campaign was started to highlight the fact that the gay couple on Modern Family had actually never kissed on the show. In September 2010, the first episode which had Mitch and Cam kiss in the background was aired, making it the first time a gay couple kissed on primetime television.

9. Haley's TV family is much like her real family

During the farewell featurette, actor Sarah Hyland revealed that her fiance Wells Adams not only asked her parents for her hand in marriage but also tracked down Julie Bowen and Ty Burrell to ask for their blessings.

10. Who are they talking to?

The Modern Family viewers have always wondered, who are all these people talking to as they give interviews? Co-creator Christopher Lloyd spoke about this in an interview to Archive of American Television. He revealed that the original plan had a Dutch filmmaker who had lived with the Pritchetts as an exchange student in his youth and had now come back to make a movie on his 'American family'. At the time, the show was titled My American Family. The makers found this tool to be too cumbersome so the filmmaker character was dropped but the documentary style was retained.

100 Q&A

1 How many seasons did "Modern Family" air?

Answer: 11

"Modern Family" first aired in the United States on September 23, 2009. The two-part "Finale" was shown on April 8, 2020, for a total of eleven years, with 250 episodes.

2 In the pilot episode, Phil describes himself as 'the cool dad'. Which of the following is not one the things he lists as a reason for this title?

- He texts
- He surfs the web
- He knows all the dances to "High School Musical"
- He can skate

Answer: He can skate

Yep. "We're all in this together! Yes we are, we're all stars, that means something, you know it...!"

3 What is Gloria's native country?

Answer: Colombia

Gloria's home town is Colombia's murder capital. She is fiercely proud of her heritage.

4 What does Dylan give Haley for Valentine's Day that Phil feels trumps his Valentine's Day gift to Claire?

Answer: A large portrait made from a photograph of the two of them

Phil always takes Claire to Fortelli's Family Style Italian Restaurant for Valentine's Day. Phil now feels he has to up the ante with Claire and suggests getting a hotel room for the evening.

5 In "Strangers on a Treadmill," Claire needed a way to tell Phil that he wasn't funny, so she asked Mitchell to do it for her, and in exchange she agreed to help Mitchell break some sensitive news to Cameron. What did Claire have to tell Cameron?

Answer: That he should stop wearing bicycle

shorts

While Claire was able to tell Cameron that he didn't look good in bicycle shorts, which clearly devastated him, Mitchell was a big wuss and bailed on his obligation to tell Phil that he wasn't funny. To make matters worse, Mitchell went so far as to tell Phil that he was hilarious and "this generation's Richard Pryor."

6 When the family headed out to Jackson Hole, Wyoming, in the season's first episode, many of the characters received cowboy nicknames from Hank, the head cowboy of the Lost Creek Ranch. Which of the following was NOT one of the given nicknames?

- Manny was "Hollywood"
- Phil was "Buffalo Phil"
- Claire was "Bossy"
- Gloria was "Desert Primrose"

Answer: Gloria was "Desert Primrose"

Gloria's nickname was actually "Cactus Flower",

which she was called throughout the episode as Hank was constantly hitting on her and trying to woo her. When he was eventually confronted by Jay, who he had dubbed as "Old Timer", he said that he had only pursued Gloria so that Jay could show up and be the hero. However, it was Phil that was the hero, as Jay was incapable of riding a horse and needed Phil's assistance to get to Gloria in order to save her from 'the horny cowboy', as Phil named him on the way home.

7 What type of animal has Luke kissed on the mouth, according to Phil?

Answer: Pigeon

In order to avoid getting a cold from Claire and Hayley, Luke decides to wear an space helmet. When Phil sees this, he says, "You care about germs, I've seen you kiss a pigeon on the mouth."

8 Who acts as Manny's father, Javier Delgado?

Answer: Benjamin Bratt

Benjamin Bratt acts as Manny's father, Javier Delgado, debuting in the episode "Up All Night".

Some of Bratt's other work includes "Law & Order", "Private Practice" and multiple other roles in television and movies. Ty Burrell acts as Phil Dunphy in the show and Ed O'Neill acts as Jay Pritchett, Manny's step father. George Lopez is a noted American talk-show host and comedian.

9 What was the name of the friend Cam and Mitchell called for a night out?

Answer: Sal

Cam and Mitchell were in Lily's room and they were talking about diapers. Cam said he couldn't tell if Lily had gone to the bathroom because the diaper was so thick. The two then realized they needed a night out with no baby talk. They both decided to call their friend, Sal.

Sal was a party girl the guys used to hang out with before Lily came along. She bet the guys she wouldn't make out with the waitresses at the bar. Sal was played by funny woman Elizabeth Banks.

10 What is the name of Jay's first wife, who is also Claire and Mitchell's mom?

Answer: DeDe

DeDe, played by actress Shelley Long, appeared in the episode "The Incident".

11 What is the name of the woman Claire introduces her husband to?

Answer: Desiree

Claire, Phil, and Luke are all out riding their bikes in their neighborhood. Desiree jogs by and stops to talk to Claire. Claire forgets Desiree's name until she reminds her. Claire continues to ride by Desiree, but stops when Desiree says hi to Phil. Claire clearly does not like Desiree, but still introduces her family to her. Phil asks Desiree where she lives and she tells him which house. Phil goes into great detail in describing the house to Desiree. Claire is looking Desiree up and down while Phil is talking to Desiree. Desiree seems uneasy about Phil knowing so much about her house until Phil tells her he is a realtor and his company represented her house.

12 What continent did Cam and Mitchell adopt their daughter from?

Answer: Asia

We first see Mitchell and Cameron in the airport. They have just arrived home from Vietnam with their daughter. Mitchell did not inform his family that they were adopting a daughter. Mitchell did not want to hear how his family would complain and judge him. He explains this to Cameron who understood his reasons. Cameron then informs Mitchell that the family is coming over for dinner that very night.

13 What are the names of the two main families?

Answer: Pritchett and Dunphy

Jay Pritchett, the patriarch, was played by Ed O'Neill (Al Bundy from "Married...with Children"), with wife Gloria, and stepson Manny. Jay's daughter Claire married Phil Dunphy and had three kids. Jay's son Mitchell married his partner Cameron Tucker and they adopted two children.

14 Why does Mitchell say that yellow is not Cameron's colour?

Answer: It makes him look like the sun

Cameron does not take kindly to this comment. Poor Cam.

15 Why does Gloria feel jealous of Maxine, a waitress in a local diner?

Answer: Because she has known Jay very well for years

Gloria is utterly confident of her own attractiveness and has no false modesty. In "Tableau Vivant", the 23rd episode of season 3, she experiences a strange emotion which Cam explains to her is jealousy. Apparently Gloria has never experienced this emotion before and exclaims 'Aye! My poor sisters' - presumably a reference to the fact that her sisters have always been jealous of her looks.

16 What comedian does Jay get Gloria tickets to see on Valentine night?

Answer: David Brenner

Jay gives Gloria tickets for them to see David Brenner, whom Gloria has never heard of. Jay explains that he was on Johnny Carson a hundreds times, and Gloria asks who Johnny Carson is.

17 When Cameron and Mitchell went on a juice fast, they were both emotionally overwrought because they were so incredibly hungry. When they attended Mitchell's boss' fundraising party, his boss told a story about a sea lion that had died due to ocean pollution. What was the name of the drowned sea lion whose story made Mitchell weep loudly in the middle of the party?

Answer: Snorkles

Cameron had been so extremely emotional and unpredictable throughout the entire episode that you expected it to be him to completely ruin the party. However it was Mitchell that became so incredibly upset that he ended up running into the ocean, falling over, and making a massive scene with Cameron, all of which was seen by his boss and the event attendees.

18 What is the license plate number of the car Claire puts on her sign in order to get the driver to slow down?

Answer: 2URN801

In order to get a speeding driver's attention, Claire decides to put up signs with the driver's license plate number all over the neighborhood with Phil's help.

19 What talent does Phil think his son Luke has in the episode "En Garde"?

Answer: Selling houses

In the episode "En Garde", Luke convinces a woman to buy a house that his father is trying to sell to her but when the woman brings her husband, Luke gets hurt running around the house and ruins the sale. Also in this episode Phil tries to test if Luke's talent is baseball.

20 What gift did Phil give Claire for their anniversary?

Answer: Phil gave a Claire a bracelet.

In the beginning of the episode, we saw Phil walk up the steps. As usual he tripped on the one bad step and said he had to fix it. Phil woke up Claire and told her happy anniversary. Phil told Claire to open her present. Claire found a Viewmaster inside and Phil told her to look at the pictures. Claire saw a picture of a bracelet and asked Phil why it was there. Phil then gave Claire the bracelet as her gift.

21 Jay had shirts printed that read "Haley's Comets". In what event was Haley participating?

Answer: 5K

This was mentioned in the episode "En Garde", in which Manny wins a fencing title.

22 Where is Jay taking Gloria for a few days?

Answer: Napa Valley

Manny's dad is taking him to Disneyland for a few days. Jay takes this opportunity to book a trip for him and Gloria to get away. Jay tells us that they would do more stuff like this if not for Manny being around. Gloria replies that Manny keeps them grounded. Later on in the episode, Manny's dad calls and cancels the trip. He tells Jay that he can't get away from the card game he is playing because the table is hot. Jay tells Manny that his dad had to cancel, but sent a limo so they all could go to Disneyland in it. Jay and Manny are starting to get used to each other and actually like each other in this episode.

23 What couple has been together the least amount of time?

Answer: Jay and Gloria

Jay and Gloria have been married for six months. Mitchell and Cameron have been together for 5 years. Phil and Claire have been married for 16 years. Jay and DeDe, Claire and Mitchell's parents were married for 35 years. The show revolves around the lives of this extended family. The show is produced to appear as a reality type show. A camera crew follows around the families and always catches them when their guard is down. In one scene Alex tells Phil and Claire that Luke's head is stuck in the banister again. Phil asks Claire where the baby oil is and she replies it is on the night stand. She didn't finish the word stand because she realizes they are being taped and told him to go look for it.

24 Who is Haley's husband?

Answer: Dylan Marshall

Dylan Marshall was played by Reid Ewing. The character appeared in the pilot episode and sporadically throughout the show's run. Dylan ultimately married Haley and they had twins.

25 What's the name of Jay's trusty dog butler?

Answer: Barkley

Gloria passionately dislikes Barkley, calling him 'El Diablo'. Jay eventually lends the dog to Cam and Mitch.

26 What is the name of Gloria's ventriloquist's dummy?

Answer: Uncle Grumpy

Luke and Manny find Uncle Grumpy in a suitcase when the family is having a yard sale. Gloria used him in the talent section she was in at the age of eighteen. Her ventroquilism skills are non existent and in the contest she froze completely. However she won anyway - indicating her body, she says 'Of course I won, imagine this at eighteen'. She has a refreshing lack of modesty.

27 Jay gives Gloria tickets as part of her Valentine's Day gift. Gloria hopes that Jay is finally taking her _____ dancing. Fill in the

blank.

Answer: Salsa

Gloria has no interest in seeing a comedian, especially one she's never heard of or doesn't use a mallet.

28 In "Halloween", Mitchell came to work in full costume because he thought it was something that everyone at his office did each year. When he arrived he realized he had made a terrible mistake and knew he wouldn't have time to go home and change his clothes. What was Mitchell's costume?

Answer: Spiderman

The only two other people at the office were considered idiots for dressing up and Mitchell tried to hide his costume underneath a business suit he had in the trunk of his car, despite the fact that his costume squeaked every time he moved.

When Mitchell went to the bathroom to transition out of the costume and into his work clothes, the janitor threw out his shirt and he ended up climbing down the drain pipe outside of the building before setting off several car alarms and making a huge scene in front of his boss and all of his coworkers.

29 Claire was determined to get a stop sign in their neighborhood and since Councilman Duane Bailey refused to do so, she decided to run for town council herself. On top of being a councilman, Duane Bailey also spoke extensively about his side business as what kind of a dog breeder?

Answer: puggle

Duane Bailey couldn't stop talking about how much we loved puggles, despite also referring to dogs as "bottomless pits of need." It not only came up when he first encountered Claire and Phil while campaigning at the grocery store, but it also came up prior to the debate when Gloria and Jay were arguing about whether their French bulldog, Stella, could be suicidal.

30 Where does it turn out Barry (played by James Marsden) is living?

Answer: Lily's princess castle

Barry, a reiki massage therapist, befriends Cameron and Mitchell, but much to their surprise, it turns out that he has been living in Lily's princess castle instead of in the upstairs apartment like Mitchell and Cameron had thought.

31 In the episode "Moon Landing", what sport are Cam and Jay playing?

Answer: Racquetball

Cam and Jay are playing racquetball. Before the game the two accidentally back into each other and their bums touch; Cam calls it a "moon landing".

32 What movie did Jay watch with his grandchildren?

Answer: The Gunfighter

Jay had a tradition of inviting the grandchildren over to spend the night. As he opened the door, he called them stinkers and told them to get in here. Luke hugged his grandfather and told him he would never forget him. Alex had told Luke earlier that day that their grandfather was going to die. Jay was of course healthy, Alex was agitating her brother.

Jay went and got a DVD for the family to watch. He picked "The Gunfighter" for the movie. Jay took Haley's shoes so she couldn't sneak off to the party three blocks away. Gloria made Jay realize he was not being fair to Haley. He went outside to where Dylan was hiding and invited him in the house. Jay told Haley she could go to the party, but had to be back by 11:00pm. Dylan saw "The Gunfighter" on the television and wanted to eat the meal that Jay had made. Haley and Dylan stayed at Jay's house and didn't go to the party.

33 Cam and Mitchell go out for a night on the town with their good friend Sal. Who plays this character?

Answer: Elizabeth Banks

All four actresses appeared as guests in season 1, however Elizabeth Banks is the actress who played Sal.

34 What name does Jay call Luke when he sees him on his sister's old bike?

Answer: Sally

The Dunphys are out riding their bikes and Phil tells Claire that Luke's still looks like a girl's bike. Claire tells Phil they will get more black tape to cover it up. The bike has black strips of tape all over it to cover all the flower decals. The bike even has a basket on it which has the number eleven on it in black tape. Phil tells the camera he is afraid Luke will be ridiculed by bullies because of the bike. We then see Jay pull up and says "Hello Sally" to Luke. Funny that Luke should be bullied by his own grandfather. Jay also says Luke looks like Little Bo Peep on his bike. Phil decides then that Luke is getting a new bike that day. This decision was news to Claire, who looks shocked when Phil said it.

35 What happens to Alex in this episode?

Answer: Luke shoots her with a BB gun.

Alex comes in the house and tell her parents Luke shot her with the gun. Luke tells Claire and Phil it was an accident. Luke starts to cry and Claire calls him and liar and tells him to stop it. Luke stops crying, as he realizes this is not going to work with his mom. Claire told Phil when he bought Luke the gun that if he ever shot someone with it then Phil would have to shoot Luke. Claire then tells Phil that he has to shoot Luke with the gun now. The family goes back and forth on a time and finally settles for 4:15pm. Luke groans and Phil tells him, sorry, it is on the calendar now.

36 What is the name of Mitch and Cam's new baby?

Answer: Rexford

In the last season, Mitch and Cam moved into a beautiful new house, complete with a karaoke room. They adopted a son and named him Rexford, after the street on which the house was located.

37 Who was scared of clowns at Luke's birthday party?

Answer: Phil

And this, by extension, meant that he was scared of Fizbo, aka Cameron. SCORPION!

38 What happens to dampen the atmosphere at Jay and Gloria's wedding reception?

Answer: Jay's ex-wife causes a scene

Although DeDe, Jay's ex, was the one who walked away from their marriage, she finds it hard to accept that Jay found someone else so quickly, especially someone as lovely as Gloria. DeDe stands up to make a speech, referencing Gloria's boobs and Jay's wallet. She is carried from the room, wrecking the wedding cake as she goes.

39 Which of the following personas does Phil NOT come up with when Claire suggests meeting at the hotel bar to see if he can pick her up?

- An honorable business man from Hong Kong
- Reginald Appleby, an English gentleman in town for a polo match
- Someone who trains tigers for a living
- Lionel Barfield, a Secret Service Agent doing fieldwork prior to the President's arrival

Answer: Lionel Barfield, a Secret Service Agent doing fieldwork prior to the President's arrival

As Phil makes each ridiculous suggestion, Claire gets more and more reluctant to go through with the scenario.

40 In "Regrets Only", Phil and Claire had awoken from the aftermath of a colossal fight, which had left Phil scratching his head as to what they had been arguing about. When rehashing the story to Gloria, he described many things he had done wrong that could have been the reason for their fight. However, which of the following was the real reason Claire exploded at him?

- Phil was supposed to bring cauliflower home and he brought broccoli, for the second straight time she had requested this
- Phil had run into a thin ex-girlfriend, Denise, and he was planning on taking her out for coffee
- Claire's friend, Debbie, called to cancel their lunch date and Phil wrote the message on a tiny slip of paper, which Claire never go, and thus she thought she had been stood up
- Phil ate a wedge salad on someone else's recommendation even though Claire suggested it to him years ago

Answer: Phil ate a wedge salad on someone else's recommendation even though Claire suggested it to him years ago

All of the items listed above were elements of their argument and while they certainly may have contributed to Phil and Claire's blowout, what truly upset Claire was the fact that Phil had taken the advice of someone else, rather than her, which made her feel like her opinion didn't matter.

41 In "Punkin Chunkin", Phil got angry at Claire for "squelching his dreams just when he's about to soar." It was then revealed that Phil fancied himself as quite an inventor, while Claire would always be the one to point out the impracticality or danger of his inventions. Which of the following WAS NOT one of Phil's failed inventions?

- Aspirin gun
- Headscratcher TM.
- Rice pudding franchise
- Toothpaste tamer

Answer: Toothpaste tamer

Every time Phil mentioned the 'Headscratcher', he

followed it up by saying 'TM', which was meant to denote the name as a trademark. After he and Claire argued about her negative attitude towards his inventions he got the 'Headscratcher' out of storage, tried it on, and ended up having a terrible experience where one of the 'patent pending rear nogginizers' started to entangle his hair inside the hat.

42 In the episode "The Old Wagon", what piece of furniture does Jay say he once built with Mitchell?

Answer: A bookshelf

Mitchell, who is not the handiest man around, reminds Jay that they once built a bookshelf together, Jays response to this is, "That was my Vietnam... and I was in Vietnam."

43 What musical instrument does Cam play?

Answer: Drums

Cam replaces a drummer in Dylan's band who is moving to Portland in the episode "Travels with Scout". At the end of the episode, the regular isn't moving to Portland anymore and Cam has to leave the band.

44 What was NOT one of the items Phil listed as a gift he would have liked to have?

Answer: Waffle Maker

Phil told us Claire was a lousy gift giver. Claire thought Phil was hard to shop for because he never asked for anything. Phil then started a long list of things he wanted. He named the watch, the speakers, and the yogurt maker as things he wanted. He said he couldn't stop listing things that he wanted.

Claire was not a great gift giver according to Phil. She gave him coupons for 5 free hugs for their anniversary. Phil tried to be excited, but he said coupons weren't for things that were usually free.

45 What is the name of the singing ensemble that Cam once ran?

Answer: The Greensleevers

The Greensleevers kicked Cam out of the group and are now singing as The New Greensleevers. As a sidenote, Bacon in the Foreground is a band name that Phil created (this is a deleted scene from the season 1 DVD set).

46 What was the name of the bike shop that Phil gets Luke's bike from?

Answer: Palms Cycle

Phil is outside of the shop talking to Luke about the responsibility of owning a bike. Phil tells Luke to not disappoint him and his mom and take good care of the bike. Earlier in the episode, Claire tells us that Luke is not ready to own his own bike. She mentions the digital camera he ruined by taking pictures of himself underwater. Phil is walking down the street and sees what he thinks is Luke's bike unlocked sitting on a street. Phil takes Luke's bike inside in order to teach him a lesson.

47 What is the name of the store Brenda works at?

Answer: Foto Fun

Manny gets Gloria and Jay to take him to the mall. Manny is there to tell Brenda how he feels about her. Manny has picked some flowers and wrote a poem for Brenda. Jay tries to save Manny from having his feelings hurt and offers Manny fifty dollars not to do it. Manny tells Jay he is eleven - what is he going to do with fifty dollars? Jay then asked Manny what he was going to do with a sixteen year old. Manny comes back a short time later and tells Gloria and Jay that Brenda has a boyfriend. He says he gave her his heart and she gave him a picture of him dressed like an old time sheriff with a mustache.

48 Alex's job is taking her to which country?

Answer: Switzerland

Alexandria Anastasia "Alex" Dunphy, played by Ariel Winter, was the often overlooked middle child and "the smart one". She gets a high-paying prestigious job but leaves it for a more philanthropic one which winds up being relocated to Switzerland.

49 Who is Phil's sexy alter ego for roleplay with Claire?

Answer: Clive Bixby

In order to spice things up on Valentine's day, Claire decided that Phil should pretend to "pick her up" at a hotel as strangers. Phil created the charming alter ego,

Clive Bixby. It was all going so well until an incident involving a dress, an elevator and public nudity changed things.

50 Poor Gloria doesn't have much luck at her weddings. What happened to disturb her wedding to her first husband?

Answer: Colombian drug dealers broke in and assassinated the judge

Gloria references this when commenting on DeDe's scene at her first wedding - 'At my first wedding, Colombian drug dealers broke in and assassinated the judge. This was way worse.

51 Manny writes a poem to Fiona to meet him at his favorite restaurant that he rhymes with a geographic feature in North America. What is this restaurant?

Answer: Great Shakes

Manny writes a poem to Fiona that tells her to meet him at Great Shakes on Valentine night, but Ted Dirkaz, who takes credit for the poem, will be there instead. Manny rhymes Great Shakes with "Great

Lakes" in his poem.

52 In "Mother's Day", Claire and Gloria took the kids on a hike but they spent the entire time whining, complaining, and fighting with each other. As a gift to themselves, Claire and Gloria left them behind and went on with the hike without them. Once they reached the top they decided to vent their frustrations about their kids, which was going fantastically well until Manny overheard one of Gloria's criticisms of him. What did Gloria say that had offended and upset Manny?

Answer: Gloria said his poetry was not very good.

After commenting that it bothered her that Manny was 'persnickety' and that he never wanted to go outside and be a 'regular boy...throw a ball or steal something', she took an opportunity to yell aloud that Manny's poetry was "not very good".

Once confronted by Manny, Claire tried to explain everything to him in an adult manner, which he seemed to understand, but Gloria decided to tell Manny that it was all a lie, it was all Claire's fault, that his poetry was fantastic, and that he was perfect in every way. While this did patch up their fight, it certainly wasn't a great moment in 'healthy parenting'.

53 In "Tableau Vivant", Alex involved the entire family in a school art project, asking them all to pose as a characters in a recreated "living portrait." Unfortunately for Alex, everyone in the family was fighting with one another over something that had happened earlier in the day. Which of the following was NOT one of the family conflicts that day?

- Luke received a medal for putting out a fire that he started at school
- Phil fired Mitchell from his real estate firm
- Claire lectured Cam on parenting and then played a cruel prank on him with the garbage disposal
- Jay told Gloria that he couldn't stand her singing

Answer: Jay told Gloria that he couldn't stand her singing

Jay has kept his mouth shut on his wife's singing and on her odd taste for offal meats and Colombian delicacies. Jay and Gloria's fight in this episode began with Gloria's jealousy of Maxine, a waitress at the diner selling the new "Jay Pritchett" sandwich. The fight was heightened when he told Gloria that it bothered her that she was so loud, which she did not appreciate whatsoever.

In the art project, the family was recreating "Freedom from Want" by Norman Rockwell, which involved a family sitting around the Thanksgiving table as the matriarch held the turkey at the end of the table.

54 According to Mitchell and Cameron, what does a PB & J stand for in their house?

Answer: Pear, brie and jambon

In order to show Cameron he is a supportive boyfriend, Mitchell decides to bring Cameron his favorite sandwich to the play rehearsal.

55 When Cam becomes the working parent and Mitchell stays at home to look after Lily, what job does Cam take up?

Answer: Greeting card salesperson

Cam sells greeting cards when Mitchell quits his job

at a law firm and looks after Lily at home. Secretly Cam hates working and wants to be with Lily and Mitchell is the other way around; this is discovered in the episode "Benched".

56 When the grandchildren came over to Jay and Gloria's house, what did Jay make them for dinner?

Answer: Sloppy Joes

Jay talked about the tradition of bringing the grandchildren over. He said they would all dress in their pajamas, eating sloppy joes and watch a western on video. Jay didn't call them sloppy joes, he called them sloppy jays. He did this because it amused him and the grandchildren.

57 In the season finale, to which professional athlete does Phil pose an awkward question?

Answer: Kobe Bryant

The awkward question was "Do you like being a basketball player guy?"

58 What kind of animal does Gloria relate Jay and

Manny to?

Answer: Burro

Gloria has a plan to get Jay and Manny to like each other. She tells us in her country when two burros don't like each other, they tie them to the same cart. She is making Jay and Manny put up a ceiling fan in Manny's room. She tells us they are the burros and the fan is the cart.

59 What is the name of the guy that hit on Gloria?

Answer: Josh

Gloria is pacing back and forth as Manny plays in his soccer match. Jay is sitting right next to Gloria in a low lawn chair. A mother of another player tells the coach to take Manny out and Gloria tells her she will take her out. Gloria tells the mom that her son spent the first part of the game with his hand down his pants. Josh then comes up and introduces himself to Gloria. He tells her he has wanted to tell the other mother off all season. He then asks Gloria if Jay is her father and Jay tells Josh he is her husband. Jay tries to get out of the chair to stand next to Gloria.

60 In which state will Luke be going to college?

Answer: Oregon

Luke Dunphy, the youngest child and goofy son, was played by Nolan Gould. He was portrayed an underachiever, and originally lied to his family about not being accepted to college. In the "Finale" he tells the family that he was accepted and will be attending college in Oregon.

61 What is Claire's original anniversary gift for Phil in the episode 'Great Expectations'?

Answer: Coupons for free hugs

Yep, bit of a trick question really. Claire did eventually bring Spandau Ballet to their living room, but it was only after she disappointed Phil with coupons.

62 Which of the following jobs did Gloria do before marrying Jay?

- School bus driver
- Train driver
- Driving instructor
- Taxi driver

Answer: Taxi driver

As a single mother, Gloria used to drive a taxi with a young Manny asleep in the footwell of the passenger seat. Rather worryingly, she is not a great driver, being very impatient of other traffic.

63 Cam explains to Manny that Valentine's Day is not the day that you run away from love. According to Cam, which of the following is NOT what Valentine's Day is the day to do to love?

- Track it down
- Tie it up
- Take it home
- Treat it gently

Answer: Treat it gently

Cam convinces Mitchell and Manny to go to Great Shakes and help Manny win back Fiona Gunderson from Ted Dirkas. At the restaurant, Mitchell comes to

Manny's defense and uses the closing argument that he was denied earlier in the day (after his client settled) on Dirkas. When Fiona still wants Dirkas instead of Manny, Manny says "This chick is crazy" and he, Cam, Mitchell, and Lily depart the restaurant.

64 In "Slow Down Your Neighbors", Jay (and eventually Luke) taught Gloria how to ride a bike, despite the fact that Gloria had many fears associated with bicycling. Beyond the obvious fears of falling down and looking foolish, what was Gloria's main reason for fearing riding her bike?

Answer: She was afraid someone was going to grab her.

Gloria's mother never let her learn how to ride a bike because she said that it was the easiest way for "people to grab you". When Manny first got on his bike, Gloria saw a neighbor near him and yelled, "Jay, he is going to grab him!"

Luke taught Gloria to ride by shooting her with a water gun to make her forget her fears and make her just "do it" and ride the bike. Once she got going Gloria really enjoyed herself. Unfortunately Claire was down the road stalking the neighborhood for a speeder, and Gloria's worst fear of someone "grabbing her" was realized when she came across Claire, who grabbed her and stole her bike to chase down the speeder.

65 In "Express Christmas", everyone was given a task and told to meet at the Dunphy house for a family celebration. Each person's day was fraught with problems and disappointments. Which of the following was NOT something the family experienced?

- Christmas tree was run over after it flew off of Mitchell's car
- Phil's mint-condition Joe DiMaggio baseball card for Jay was destroyed after Manny hit him with the stun gun
- Gloria destroyed the Christmas tree angel when she threw it out the car window after she noticed a spider on it
- Cameron threw his back out when he fell into Jay's pool while carrying the presents

Answer: Cameron threw his back out when he fell into Jay's pool while carrying the presents

My favorite moment of this episode was when Gloria went to help Luke find the angel in the attic and discovered that Jay was hiding Barkley, the dog butler, up there, which she thought was the devil and vehemently wanted out of the house in the show's first season.

The episode and the family's Christmas was saved in the end when Jay convinced everyone to go and get Chinese food, only for them to open the door and discover he had hired a snow machine to decorate the front of the house.

66 Who does the man Phil sprayed with cologne turn out to be?

Answer: Longines

When Phil gets angry with Jay at the mall, he takes his anger out on the perfume guy, who just happens to be Mitchell and Cameron's friend Longines.

67 What is the name of the burgers Jay makes on Jay's night?

Answer: Sloppy Jays

Jay makes these burgers especially for Jay's Night where all his grandchildren come over for the night. This features in the episode "Great Expectations".

68 Who did Sal refer to as her baby cub?

Answer: Mitchell

Sal was extremely excited to see both Mitchell and Cam. She greeted Cam first as her big bear. Then she ran to Mitchell and called him her baby cub. The three of them had partied a great deal before Cam and Mitchell adopted Lily. We saw picture of the three of them, intoxicated, at a New Year's Eve party. Mitchell was wearing eyeglasses that had the year 2005 on them.

69 Manny lost his valentine because his poem was stolen by another kid. What was the name of this kid?

Answer: Ted Durkas

Ted Durkas was also mentioned in the episode where Manny and Luke got into a fight at school.

70 What movie made Cam upset in this episode?

Answer: "Sophie's Choice"

Cam is extremely distraught over the movie; he cries at the end of the episode. He tries to explain the movie to us and the difficult decision Sophie had to make. Cam explains he doesn't know what he would do if he had to choice between Lily and Mitchell. He runs out of the room crying, saying he doesn't know what he would do.

71 What Elton John song is playing when Cameron presents Lily to the family?

Answer: "The Circle of Life"

Mitchell has been trying to tell the family the news of the adoption. Jay makes a comment about Cameron being dramatic. Mitchell was trying to defend his boyfriend against this comment when the lights suddenly dim and the song came on. Cameron, much like the scene in "The Lion King", was carrying Lily held out in the air like Simba was presented to his kingdom by Rafiki. Mitchell tells Cameron to turn it off and Cameron says he can't, that this is who he is. Mitchell tells Cameron he meant the song.

72 What is the name of Jay and Gloria's youngest

son?

Answer: Joe

Jay's stepson Manny Delgado, is the biological son of Gloria and her ex-husband Javier. In the fourth season of "Modern Family", in the episode "Party Crasher", Jay and Gloria have a son who they name Fulgencio Joseph "Joe" Pritchett. He was born just after midnight on Manny's fourteenth birthday.

73 What was the name of the caroling group Cameron got kicked out of?

Answer: The Greensleevers

It was his Dreamgirls. He was Effy.

74 What are the aliases that Phil and Claire use when they meet in the bar?

Answer: Clive and Julianna

Phil is wearing a nametag that says his alias is Clive. Claire asks if he's in for a convention or does he forget his name a lot.

75 In "Unplugged", the Dunphy family competed to see who could go the longest without using any electronic devices, such as cell phones, computers, video games, or the internet. Who was the winner of the contest?

Answer: Haley

Luke was out first, as he ran to the computer after his friend told him of a parasailing donkey video on Youtube. Alex conceded because she needed the internet for her homework and Claire was caught cheating and using the computer to book plane tickets.

The final two competitors were Phil and Haley. Haley tricked them into thinking she was talking on her cell phone just long enough for Phil to break and use the computer, which is when she revealed to the family that she hadn't been on her cell phone, but rather had been talking into a black bar of soap she had turned into a phone replica. Unfortunately for Haley they had no intention of buying her a car if she won, so there ended up not being any reward.

76 On "Leap Day", we found out that Cameron

was a leap day baby and was officially turning 10 (or 40, if you asked Mitchell). In honor of his birthday, Mitchell had organized a fantastic theme party focused around Cameron's favorite film. While he ended up having to cancel and rework everything on short notice, what movie provided the original party theme?

Answer: Wizard of Oz

Mitchell told Cameron it was a 'simple party' but then described it as an "Oz themed extravaganza, with yellow brick carpet, waitstaff in full costume, and custom-made ruby slippers for Cam! Whazzup!"

Unfortunately for Mitchell, Cam reminded him of the recent tragedy in his family which involved a massive tornado devastating his grandfather's farm. It was this that caused Mitchell to change the theme and resulted in a failed party. The day was saved, however, when Mitchell finally realized that Cam was just upset about was turning 40, so they decided to go to the carnival and act like a couple of 10 year old kids.

77 What is the name of the film Claire and Phil want to see in the episode "Our Children

Ourselves"?

Answer: Croctopus in 3D

After questioning themselves as parents, Phil and Claire decide to go see the movie "Croctopus in 3D". When they are about to walk into the theater however, they see the parents of Alex's rival (Sanjay Patel) walk into a French movie, so they decide to watch it as well, much to Phil's disappointment.

78 What is the name of Claire's old work friend?

Answer: Valerie

Claire meets her old work friend Valerie in the episode "Moon Landing".

79 What type of daiquiri was Mitchell drinking at the bar?

Answer: Passion fruit

Sal had asked the boys if they noticed anything different about her. They asked her if she got her haircut or her teeth whitened. She said no and then opened her jacket. Sal had gotten a boob job. She asked Mitchell if he wanted to touch them and he said he was gay, not buried. Mitchell asked Cam if he minded and he said no. Cam said Mitchell was drinking passion fruit daiquiris so he could do whatever he wanted. As the night progressed the threesome got drunk on the daiquiris and tequila shots.

80 When Claire and Phil are role playing, what is Phil's name?

Answer: Clive Bixby

He is wearing a name tag that reads "Hello. My name is Clive Bixby".

81 Who is the first person we see at the beginning of the episode?

Answer: Jay

Jay is sitting on the couch contemplating what it means to be a parent, or more specifically, a father. He is thinking about his answer when the camera goes to Phil then to Cam and Mitchell. The funniest part of this segment is when Phil gives three different answers and Claire says they are all wrong. Phil then tells Claire to just give him the answer.

82 Who plays the role of Phil Dunphy?

Answer: Ty Burrell

Phil plays the role of the dad who thinks he is cool. Phil is actually kind of an air head when it comes to things. He tries to make his three children think of him as a friend. The only one of the kids that does is his son, Luke. Luke is just like his dad, an airhead. In one of his interviews, Phil tells us that he knows all the cool 'texting verbage'. He says that WTF means 'what the face'. He then says he knows all the words to "High School Musical". We see him performing as his kids look on horrified.

83 What job will Cam be taking?

Answer: football coach

While Cam has been a music teacher and Fizbo the clown, he was originally turned down for his dream job as a football coach in his Missouri home town. After just moving to a new home and adopting a son, Cam gets a call telling him that the current coach was found drunk and fired. He was offered the job and, after some soul-searching and discussions with Mitch, he decides to take it.

84 What sport did Mitchell and Claire perform together as kids?

Answer: Figure skating

Mitch and Claire's figure skating duo was christened "Fire and Ice". Mitch was Fire, because of his hair, Claire was Ice, because she was really mean.

85 What was Gloria's attitude to Manny when he was a baby?

Answer: She sometimes dressed him as a girl

Although Gloria loves Manny, she would have liked to have had a girl to dress up. She used to dress Manny as a girl, but stopped because she didn't want him to grow up 'messed up'. When he asks who the little girl is in old photographs, Gloria tells him that it is his twin sister who died!

Gloria's figure pinged right back into shape after she

gave birth to her second son, so it's not likely that her pregnancy with Manny marred her figure.

86 Claire asks Phil (in character) "So if your wife is so beautiful, why are you here with me?" What is Claire's response when Phil tells her that he respects his wife too much to do the things he's going to do to her?

Answer: "Oh, jackpot"

Claire lets Phil have a redo after he heads down the path that his wife is always tired and makes endless lists for him to do. Claire is much more pleased with his second attempt.

87 In "Good Cop Bad Dog", Cameron was extremely sick and needed Mitchell to take care of him, even though it was on the same day they were supposed to see what famous singer?

Answer: Lady Gaga

Mitchell spent the entire episode trying to justify going to the concert without Cameron, and even worse, going to the concert without even telling him that he planned to do so. While he went back and forth on his decision, the last segment of the show revealed that he had attended the show while Cameron slept on the couch. What gave Mitchell away was the flashing light necklace hidden under his polo shirt that he had forgotten to remove before coming back home.

88 In "Send Out the Clowns", Cameron was reunited with many of his clown college friends at the funeral of their former 'Professor Ringmaster Al Uzielli'. As they buried him each clown took a turn reenacting a classic 'clown' technique upon the professor's grave. Which of the following was NOT one of the clown moves?

- Dropping a pie onto the casket
- Stumbling and dumping a bucket of confetti on to the casket
- Throwing an alarm clock bomb onto the casket
- Spraying a silly string fire extinguisher onto the casket

Answer: Spraying a silly string fire extinguisher onto the casket

Cameron was reunited with his former clowning

partner Louis, of "Louis and Fizbo" fame. After Cam stayed out late and came home extremely drunk doing spit takes all over the kitchen, Cam and Louis decided to put the group together again for a child's birthday party. While Cameron meant it to be a one-time event, Louis got the impression it was going to be a permanent thing going forward. Once the truth was revealed, Louis did not take it well at all and ended up attacking Cam during their routine at the party.

89 What is the name of the man Mitchell mistakes for his son?

Answer: Bobby

After seeing a red haired person with his ex-girlfriend, Mitchell thinks that the person is his son. Instead, it is his ex-girlfriend's husband.

90 What is the name of Cam's clown character?

Answer: Fizbo

Cam's first appearance as Fizbo the clown is in the episode titled "Fizbo", where he dresses up as Fizbo for Luke's birthday party.

91 Where were Mitchell and Cam going to go with their friend for vacation?

Answer: Cabo

Sal wanted the guys to go on vacation with her. She said they had been talking about going to Cabo for a long time and they should do it. Cam and Mitchell got just as excited as Sal. They said they were going to bring Lily along with them. Sal then said that she wanted to drown Lily in the ocean. The guys had to do a double take when they heard this. They both came to realize Sal was jealous of Lily.

92 Jay brought home a dog butler statue from Las Vegas. What is the name of this creature which Gloria despises?

Answer: Barkley

This is from the episode "Not in My House".

93 What is the name of the gay couple Cam and Mitchell meet at the day care center?

Answer: Anton and Scott

Through the whole episode, Mitchell asks Cam not to act gay. He does not want anyone to judge their daughter for them being gay. Cam does as Mitchell asks and then Anton and Scott come in. The women at the center all get excited when they see the two guys. Cam tells Mitchell he could have cleaned up with this crowd. Mitchell allows Cam to dance and he outshines Anton and Scott easily.

94 What is Gloria's village being recognized as number one for?

Answer: murder

Jay and Gloria are sitting on the couch and talking about some of the things that make them different from each other. Gloria is extremely proud of her Colombian heritage. She tells us that her little village is number one. She is not sure what the word is so she asks Jay. Jay tells her the word is murder and Gloria repeats it proudly.

95 What country is Lily from?

Answer: Vietnam

Lily Tucker-Pritchett was born in Vietnam on

February 19th 2008. She was adopted by Cam and Mitch as an infant. She has been played by Aubrey Anderson Emmons who, literally, grew up on the show.

96 Where is Cameron from?

Answer: Missouri

Although he "screams Hawaii", Cam was born and raised on a farm in Missouri. And Missourahh's more cosmopolitan than you may think, it has a very vibrant cowboy poetry scene.

97 Claire gets the belt of her coat caught in the escalator. Why is this a big deal?

Answer: Because she is naked underneath the coat

Claire excuses herself from Phil at the bar and she goes and removes all of her clothes and returns to the bar dressed only in her coat. As she and Phil are going upstairs to the hotel room, the belt gets caught in the escalator and Claire is horrified, especially when people she and Phil know recognize them.

98 In "Someone to Watch Over Lily," Mitchell and Cameron were trying to decide who they should choose as guardian of Lily if they were to die unexpectedly. While Phil and Claire were their first choice, they decided to go with Jay and Gloria. Which of the following was NOT one of the reasons they decided Phil and Claire were not the right choice?

- They stopped by and all of the Dunphys were yelling at each other and the fry pan kept catching fire
- Phil and Claire forgot Luke in a parking garage after a child psychologist appointment
- Alex and Haley were arrested for breaking into their high school
- Phil was arrested for lewd behavior on Valentine's day

Answer: Phil was arrested for lewd behavior on Valentine's day

Phil was detained by the police on Valentine's day in the "Bixby's Back" episode of this season when he accidentally went into the wrong hotel room to wait for Claire on their 'romantic night out.'

Mitch and Cam questioned whether Gloria and Jay were the right choice because Gloria had pierced Lily's ears behind their back and they had just witnessed Jay bullying Manny at a sporting goods store. Gloria and Jay did end up being Mitch and Cam's choice for guardians, despite the fact that Gloria was far too excited and optimistic about becoming Lily's mother when something terrible happened to Mitch and Cam.

99 When Luke's friend, Walt, passed away, it became Claire and Phil's responsibility to tell him and help him cope with the loss. While Claire was profoundly upset by Luke's lack of response to Walt's death, Phil was completely freaked out by Claire's "bad news" defense mechanism. What does Claire do when she gives people very bad news?

Answer: She smiles

It was actually Phil that was the nervous blinker, as we found out in "Tableau Vivant" when he had to fire Mitchell from working with his real estate firm.

When Claire gave people the news of Walt's death she

couldn't stop herself from "smiling like the Joker" and it made everyone even more upset.

100 What is the name of the restaurant Mitchell and Cameron go to in "Caught in the Act"?

Answer: Shawarma City

In order to try something new, other than Shawarma City, Mitchell and Cameron try to befriend the owner of the newest restaurant in town. That doesn't quite work out for Cameron and Mitchell, so they decide to go back to Shawarma City.

Printed in Great Britain
by Amazon

72234549R00040